365 Knock-Knock Jokes

365 Knock-Knock Jokes

By Robert Myers

Drawings by Eileen N. Toohey

BARNES & NOBLE BOOKS
NEW YORK

This edition published by Barnes & Noble, Inc.,
by arrangement with Robert Myers.

Copyright © 1995 by Robert Myers

1995 Barnes & Noble Books

Book design by James Sarfati

Drawings by Eileen N. Toohey

ISBN 1-56619-601-9

Printed and bound in the United States of America

M 9 8 7 6 5 4 3 2

To the memory of my father

Joseph W. Myers

Knock, knock.
Who's there?
Myer.
Myer who?
Myer in a good mood today.

Knock, knock.
Who's there?
Who.
Who who?
I didn't know you stuttered.

Knock, knock.
Who's there?
Hammond.
Hammond who?
Hammond eggs
    with toast is delicious.

Knock, knock.
Who's there?
Rhonda.
Rhonda who?
Rhonda arrest!

Knock, knock.
Who's there?
Zoom.
Zoom who?
Zoom do you think?

Knock, knock.
Who's there?
Concha.
Concha who?
Concha come out and play?

Knock, knock.
Who's there?
Dora Belle.
Dora Belle who?
Dora Belle is broken—that's why I knocked.

Knock, knock.
Who's there?
Typhoid.
Typhoid who?
Typhoid that question before.

Knock, knock.
Who's there?
Harold.
Harold who?
Harold do you think I am?

Knock, knock.
Who's there?
Yeast.
Yeast who?
Yeast you can do is laugh at this joke.

Knock, knock.
Who's there?
Tibet.
Tibet who?
You want Tibet on who it is?

Knock, knock.
Who's there?
Argo.
Argo who?
Argo fly a kite!

Knock, knock.
Who's there?
Theresa.
Theresa who?
Theresa fly in my soup.

Knock, knock.
Who's there?
Beth.
Beth who?
Beth wishes on your graduation.

Knock, knock.
Who's there?
Harris.
Harris who?
Harris your book report coming?

Knock, knock.
Who's there?
Sacha.
Sacha who?
Sacha clown! Doesn't my face
   look familiar?

Knock, knock.
Who's there?
Jewel.
Jewel who?
Jewel be happy to know that I passed my math test.

Knock, knock.
Who's there?
Aurora.
Aurora who?
Aurora is what a lion does.

Knock, knock.
Who's there?
Omega.
Omega who?
Omega up your mind.

Knock, knock.
Who's there?
Lyndon.
Lyndon who?
Lyndon ear, and I'll tell you a secret.

Knock, knock.
Who's there?
Meg.
Meg who?
Meg up your mind.

Knock, knock.
Who's there?
Hollis.
Hollis who?
Hollis forgiven. You're still my friend.

Knock, knock.
Who's there?
Formosa.
Formosa who?
Formosa the winter I stayed indoors.

Knock, knock.
Who's there?
Shad.
Shad who?
Shad stories make me cry.

Knock, knock.
Who's there?
Eiffel.
Eiffel who?
Eiffel off my bike and hurt my leg.

Knock, knock.
Who's there?
Bob.
Bob who?
Bob baa black sheep, have you any wool?

Knock, knock.
Who's there?
Abyssinia.
Abyssinia who?
Abyssinia in my dreams.

Knock, knock.
Who's there?
Toulouse.
Toulouse who?
Want Toulouse weight? Stop eating candy.

Knock, knock.
Who's there?
Sinbad.
Sinbad who?
Sinbad and you'll never get to heaven.

Knock, knock.
Who's there?
Ida.
Ida who?
Ida you let me in or I'm telling your parents.

Knock, knock.
Who's there?
Mandy.
Mandy who?
Mandy battle stations! Here comes the enemy!

Knock, knock.
Who's there?
Cosmo.
Cosmo who?
You Cosmo trouble
    than anyone I know.

Knock, knock.
Who's there?
Ardley.
Ardley who?
I Ardley know you, but let's be friends.

Knock, knock.
Who's there?
Kenya.
Kenya who?
Kenya please keep quiet in there.
    I'm trying to sleep.

Knock, Knock.
Who's there?
Cynthia.
Cynthia who?
Cynthia been a good kid,
    here's some candy.

Knock, knock.
Who's there?
Annette.
Annette who?
Annette is used to catch fish.

10

Knock, knock.
Who's there?
El.
El who?
El low. How are you?

Knock, knock.
Who's there?
Dodson.
Dodson who?
Dodson old joke,
    really old.

Knock, knock.
Who's there?
Verdi.
Verdi who?
Verdi good question.
    It's me.

Knock, knock.
Who's there?
Dewey.
Dewey who?
Dewey have to do our homework tonight?

Knock, knock.
Who's there?
Joanne.
Joanne who?
Joanne tell is a fun game.

Knock, knock.
Who's there?
Hallways.
Hallways who?
Hallways had a feeling you didn't like me.

Knock, knock.
Who's there?
Veal.
Veal who?
Veal look for that lost ball now.

Knock, knock.
Who's there?
Esther.
Esther who?
Esther anything I can pick up for you at the store?

Knock, knock.
Who's there?
Melissa.
Melissa who?
Melissa to you and
    I'll really get in trouble.

Knock, knock.
Who's there?
Iowa.
Iowa who?
Iowa a lot. She saved my life.

Knock, knock.
Who's there?
Duress.
Duress who?
Duress looks good on you.
   Is it new?

Knock, knock.
Who's there?
Mile.
Mile who?
'Mile, I'm going to take your picture.

Knock, knock.
Who's there?
Ohio.
Ohio who?
Ohio Silver!

Knock, knock.
Who's there?
Torch.
Torch who?
Torch you would never ask.

Knock, knock.
Who's there?
Hyman.
Hyman who?
Hyman the mood for Chinese food.

Knock, knock.
Who's there?
Yoga.
Yoga who?
Yoga the best friend
    in the world—me!

Knock, knock.
Who's there?
Sawyer.
Sawyer who?
Sawyer at the car wash yesterday.

Knock, knock.
Who's there?
Aldo.
Aldo who?
Aldo my room after dinner.

Knock, knock.
Who's there?
Disk.
Disk who?
Disk must be the place.

Knock, knock.
Who's there?
Toyota.
Toyota who?
Toyota be a law against these silly jokes.

Knock, knock.
Who's there?
Goliath.
Goliath who?
Goliath down.
  You look very tired.

Knock, knock.
Who's there?
Soup.
Soup who?
Soup-erman is here!

Knock, knock.
Who's there?
Walrus.
Walrus who?
Why do you Walrus
    ask that question?

Knock, knock.
Who's there?
Census.
Census who?
Census Sunday I have no homework.

Knock, knock.
Who's there?
Abbot.
Abbot who?
Abbot time you
recognized me.

Knock, knock.
Who's there?
Fish.
Fish who?
I Fish you a happy birthday.

Knock, knock.
Who's there?
Archer.
Archer who?
Archer happy to see your old friend?

Knock, knock.
Who's there?
Troy.
Troy who?
Troy to find out yourself.

Knock, knock.
Who's there?
Ate.
Ate who?
Ate, nine, ten, eleven . . .

Knock, knock.
Who's there?
Howie.
Howie who?
I'm fine. Are you O.K.?

Knock, knock.
Who's there?
Budapest.
Budapest who?
You're nothing Budapest.

Knock, knock.
Who's there?
Canoe.
Canoe who?
Canoe please stop foolin' around
    and let me in.

Knock, knock.
Who's there?
Orson.
Orson who?
Orson carriage went out
    of style many years ago.

Knock, knock.
Who's there?
Sari.
Sari who?
Sari I was sarong.

Knock, knock.
Who's there?
Horace.
Horace who?
Horace I to know
    you lived here?

Knock, knock.
Who's there?
Wanda.
Wanda who?
Wanda buy some candy?

Knock, knock.
Who's there?
Lock.
Lock who?
Lock to see who it is.

Knock, knock.
Who's there?
Cohen.
Cohen who?
Cohen home after
   I return these books.

Knock, knock.
Who's there?
Missouri.
Missouri who?
Missouri loves company.

Knock, knock.
Who's there?
Amahl.
Amahl who?
Amahl excited about tomorrow's
    trip to the zoo.

Knock, knock.
Who's there?
Yvonne.
Yvonne who?
Yvonne to know
    if your sister is home.

Knock, knock.
Who's there?
Alfie.
Alfie who?
Alfie you in school.

Knock, knock.
Who's there?
Doughnut.
Doughnut who?
Doughnut be so dumb!
    You know very well who it is.

Knock, knock.
Who's there?
Butter.
Butter who?
Butter be quick—
    the cops are after me!

Knock, knock.
Who's there?
Udall.
Udall who?
Udall know the answer
  if you opened the door.

Knock, knock.
Who's there?
House.
House who?
House soon
    can we leave for the movies?

Knock, knock.
Who's there?
Auto.
Auto who?
Auto know who I am by now.

Knock, knock.
Who's there?
Salada.
Salada who?
Salada nerve asking me
    that question again.

Knock, knock.
Who's there?
Venice.
Venice who?
Venice your dad
    coming home from the hospital?

Knock, knock.
Who's there?
Radio.
Radio who?
Radio not, here I come.

Knock, knock.
Who's there?
Lass.
Lass who?
Lass one out is a rotten egg.

Knock, knock.
Who's there?
Hop.
Hop who?
Hop you like my new jacket.

Knock, knock.
Who's there?
Vilma.
Vilma who?
Vilma grades go up if I study?

Knock, knock.
Who's there?
Yule.
Yule who?
Yule never guess.

Knock, knock.
Who's there?
Zizi.
Zizi who?
Zizi come, Zizi go.

Knock, knock.
Who's there?
Della.
Della who?
Della-katessen opens at noon today.
Let's get a sandwich.

Knock, knock.
Who's there?
Fred.
Fred who?
Fred I won't be
seeing you today.

Knock, knock.
Who's there?
Odysseus.
Odysseus who?
Odysseus your brother.

Knock, knock.
Who's there?
Wendy.
Wendy who?
Wendy telephone is fixed,
    I'll give you a call.

Knock, knock.
Who's there?
Nun.
Nun who?
Nun of your business.

Knock, knock.
Who's there?
Miniature.
Miniature who?
Miniature open this door,
    I'm rushing up to my room.

Knock, knock.
Who's there?
Weasel.
Weasel who?
Weasel while you work.

Knock, knock.
Who's there?
Eisenhower.
Eisenhower who?
Eisenhower early—is that O.K.?

Knock, knock.
Who's there?
Witch.
Witch who?
Witch name do you want to hear?

Knock, knock.
Who's there?
Toucan.
Toucan who?
Toucan live as cheaply as one.

Knock, knock.
Who's there?
Anita.
Anita who?
Anita ride home.
   Can you help?

Knock, knock.
Who's there?
Statue.
Statue who?
Statue? This is me.

Knock, knock.
Who's there?
Gladys.
Gladys who?
Gladys the weekend,
   no homework!

Knock, knock.
Who's there?
Arnold.
Arnold who?
Arnold who you are.

Knock, knock.
Who's there?
Sis.
Sis who?
Sis any way to write a book?

Knock, knock.
Who's there?
Eddie.
Eddie who?
Eddie body home?

Knock, knock.
Who's there?
Dewey.
Dewey who?
Dewey have to wipe our feet
   before we come into the house?

Knock, knock.
Who's there?
Nobel.
Nobel who?
Nobel, so I gotta knock.

Knock, knock.
Who's there?
Orange juice.
Orange juice who?
Orange juice going to stop
with these silly jokes?

Knock, knock.
Who's there?
Whittier.
Whittier who?
Whittier want to do
after the movie?

Knock, knock.
Who's there?
Gopher.
Gopher who?
Gopher a walk
and clear your head.

Knock, knock.
Who's there?
Harmony.
Harmony who?
Harmony bucks
have you got to lend me?

Knock, knock.
Who's there?
Tobias.
Tobias who?
Tobias some burgers—
    that's why I went to the supermarket.

Knock, knock.
Who's there?
Ball.
Ball who?
Ball for one and one for Ball.

Knock, knock.
Who's there?
Lyle.
Lyle who?
Lyle tell you in a minute.

Knock, knock.
Who's there?
Mary.
Mary who?
Mary Christmas and
    Happy New Year!

Knock, knock.
Who's there?
Les.
Les who?
Les go to the movies.

Knock, knock.
Who's there?
Eggs.
Eggs who?
Eggs-tremely important
    that you get a good education.

Knock, knock.
Who's there?
Lettuce.
Lettuce who?
Lettuce in and we'll be very thankful.

Knock, knock.
Who's there?
Yachts.
Yachts who?
Yachts your name?

Knock, knock.
Who's there?
Saul.
Saul who?
Saul I need is a million bucks,
    and I'll be rich.

Knock, knock.
Who's there?
Oslo.
Oslo who?
Oslo down. What's the hurry?

Knock, knock.
Who's there?
Lee.
Lee who?
Lee me alone, please.
   I don't feel well.

Knock, knock.
Who's there?
Willy.
Willy who?
Willy answer the door or not?

Knock, knock.
Who's there?
Maxie.
Maxie who?
Maxie-mum perfection
  is what you should always strive for.

Knock, knock.
Who's there?
John.
John who?
John the Little League
   and play baseball.

Knock, knock.
Who's there?
Fido.
Fido who?
Fido I have to study?
   I know it all!

Knock, knock.
Who's there?
Arthur.
Arthur who?
Arthur-itis is a terrible disease.

Knock, knock.
Who's there?
Ghana.
Ghana who?
Ghana get you if you don't open up!

Knock, knock.
Who's there?
Sid.
Sid who?
Sid down, I'll use my key.

Knock, knock.
Who's there?
Opera.
Opera who?
Opera-tunity only knocks once.

Knock, knock.
Who's there?
Desi.
Desi who?
Desi good reason
   for these knock-knock jokes.

Knock, knock.
Who's there?
Earl.
Earl who?
Earl be happy to know
   I can come out and play.

Knock, knock.
Who's there?
Oz.
Oz who?
Oz out here
   in the pouring rain.

Knock, knock.
Who's there?
Walter.
Walter who?
Walter wall carpeting
   is great for the feet.

41

Knock, knock.
Who's there?
Mickey.
Mickey who?
Mickey is stuck in the lock!

Knock, knock.
Who's there?
Moose.
Moose who?
Moose you always be so nosy?

Knock, knock.
Who's there?
Doris.
Doris who?
Doris open, mind if I visit?

Knock, knock.
Who's there?
Hugh.
Hugh who?
Yoo-hoo to you, too!

Knock, knock.
Who's there?
Swatter.
Swatter who?
Swatter you want from me?

Knock, knock.
Who's there?
Mayonnaise.
Mayonnaise who?
Mayonnaise are not
    what they used to be.

Knock, knock.
Who's there?
Stan.
Stan who?
Stan back, I'm comin' in.

Knock, knock.
Who's there?
Almond.
Almond who?
Almond your side, buddy!

Knock, knock.
Who's there?
Randall.
Randall who?
Randall the way
    home from school.

Knock, knock.
Who's there?
Tarzan.
Tarzan who?
Tarzan stripes are
    found in our flag.

Knock, knock.
Who's there?
Musket.
Musket who?
Musket in,
    this is an emergency!

Knock, knock.
Who's there?
Hair.
Hair who?
Hair comes the parade!

Knock, knock.
Who's there?
Sal.
Sal who?
Sal we dance?

Knock, knock.
Who's there?
Robin.
Robin who?
Robin banks is illegal.

Knock, knock.
Who's there?
Congo.
Congo who?
Congo on meeting you like this.
People are talking.

Knock, knock.
Who's there?
Olive.
Olive who?
Olive across the street.

Knock, knock.
Who's there?
Dennis.
Dennis who?
Dennis is pulling my tooth today.

Knock, knock.
Who's there?
Justin.
Justin who?
Justin case I don't see you,
    happy birthday!

Knock, knock.
Who's there?
Kipper.
Kipper who?
Kipper your mouth shut!

Knock, knock.
Who's there?
Whitmore.
Whitmore who?
Whitmore can I say?

Knock, knock.
Who's there?
Eliza.
Eliza who?
Eliza wake at night,
   thinking up knock-knock jokes.

Knock, knock.
Who's there?
Yucca.
Yucca who?
Yucca ask anybody who I am.

Knock, knock.
Who's there?
Aida.
Aida who?
Aida lot of hamburgers and now I'm sick.

Knock, knock.
Who's there?
Heifer.
Heifer who?
Heifer dollar
    is worth fifty cents.

Knock, knock.
Who's there?
Ridya.
Ridya who?
Ridya bike
    for great exercise.

Knock, knock.
Who's there?
Forty.
Forty who?
Forty tenth time,
   I must see your sister!

Knock, knock.
Who's there?
Russian.
Russian who?
Russian about is silly,
   slow down.

Knock, knock.
Who's there?
Owl.
Owl who?
Owl be your friend
   if you open the door.

Knock, knock.
Who's there?
Twig.
Twig who?
Twig or tweet, you turkey!

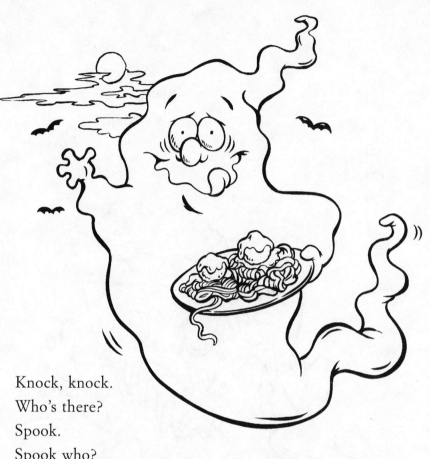

Knock, knock.
Who's there?
Spook.
Spook who?
Spook-etti with meatballs
    is my favorite food.

Knock, knock.
Who's there?
Ooze.
Ooze who?
Ooze gonna open the door?

Knock, knock.
Who's there?
Oscar.
Oscar who?
Oscar if she wants dinner.

Knock, knock.
Who's there?
Elsie.
Elsie who?
Elsie you in my dreams.

Knock, knock.
Who's there?
Cy.
Cy who?
Cy knew you were home.

Knock, knock.
Who's there?
Fitzmead.
Fitzmead who?
Fitzmead just fine, thank you.

Knock, knock.
Who's there?
Candy.
Candy who?
Candy-magine why
   you don't know who I am.

Knock, knock.
Who's there?
Thaddeus.
Thaddeus who?
Thaddeus the question, my dear Hamlet.

Knock, knock.
Who's there?
Wooden.
Wooden who?
Wooden you like to know?

Knock, knock.
Who's there?
Mischa.
Mischa who?
Mischa a lot.
    Let's get together.

Knock, knock.
Who's there?
Leggo.
Leggo who?
Leggo the door—
    I wanna come in!

Knock, knock.
Who's there?
Lisa.
Lisa who?
Lisa you can do is
    hear me out.

Knock, knock.
Who's there?
Euripedes.
Euripedes who?
Euripedes pants,
  and I'll smacka your face.

Knock, knock. ·
Who's there?
Isthmus.
Isthmus who?
Isthmus be the place!

Knock, knock.
Who's there?
Weirdo.
Weirdo who?
Weirdo you think you're going?

Knock, knock.
Who's there?
Hoppy.
Hoppy who?
Hoppy holidays
  to you and your family.

Knock, knock.
Who's there?
Chester.
Chester who?
Chester minute!
  Don't you remember who I am?

Knock, knock.
Who's there?
Zinc.
Zinc who?
Zinc of the good times
  we're gonna have on vacation.

Knock, knock.
Who's there?
Avenue.
Avenue who?
Avenue heard about
the new movie?

Knock, knock.
Who's there?
Harvard.
Harvard who?
Harvard you like me
to answer that question?

Knock, knock.
Who's there?
Cozy.
Cozy who?
Cozy who's at the back door.

Knock, knock.
Who's there?
Ketchup.
Ketchup who?
Ketchup with me if you can.

Knock, knock.
Who's there?
Atch.
Atch who?
Terrible cold you've got.

Knock, knock.
Who's there?
Wayne.
Wayne who?
Wayne drops keep falling on my head.

Knock, knock.
Who's there?
Europe.
Europe who?
Europe very early
    this morning, no?

Knock, knock.
Who's there?
Harris.
Harris who?
Harris fun to have in the winter.
    It keeps your head warm.

Knock, knock.
Who's there?
Hobbit.
Hobbit who?
Hobbit going to the hockey game?
    I've got free tickets.

Knock, knock.
Who's there?
Gucci.
Gucci who?
Gucci-Gucci-Gucci-Goo!

Knock, knock.
Who's there?
Watts.
Watts who?
Watts up, Doc?

Knock, knock.
Who's there?
Mitzi.
Mitzi who?
Mitzi last train
  and you'll have to walk home.

Knock, knock.
Who's there?
Ivor.
Ivor who?
Ivor sore hand from knocking on your door!

Knock, knock.
Who's there?
Juno.
Juno who?
Juno where the bus stops?

Knock, knock.
Who's there?
Rita.
Rita who?
Rita good book
    instead of watching cartoons!

Knock, knock.
Who's there?
Lotto.
Lotto who?
Lotto problems if you don't
    pay your bills on time.

Knock, knock.
Who's there?
Faucet.
Faucet who?
Faucet open and you're sure
    to break the doorknob.

Knock, knock.
Who's there?
Amateur.
Amateur who?
Amateur service, sir.

Knock, knock.
Who's there?
Watusi.
Watusi who?
Watusi is what you get.

Knock, knock.
Who's there?
Waiter.
Waiter who?
Waiter minute—I'm not ready yet!

Knock, knock.
Who's there?
Daisy.
Daisy who?
Daisy plays, nights he sleeps.

Knock, knock.
Who's there?
Swan.
Swan who?
Swan to go swimming
in my pool?

Knock, knock.
Who's there?
Vera.
Vera who?
Vera all my birthday gifts?

Knock, knock.
Who's there?
Liz.
Liz who?
Liz-en to me.
 I know what I'm talking about.

Knock, knock.
Who's there?
Hugh.
Hugh who?
Hugh going away
 for the Christmas holiday?

Knock, knock.
Who's there?
Halibut.
Halibut who?
Halibut going fishing on my dad's boat?

Knock, knock.
Who's there?
Wanamaker.
Wanamaker who?
Wanamaker snowman?

Knock, knock.
Who's there?
Bean.
Bean who?
Bean looking for you all day.

Knock, knock.
Who's there?
Eumenides.
Eumenides who?
Eumenides pants so I can wear them.

Knock, knock.
Who's there?
Siam.
Siam who?
Siam your next door neighbor.

Knock, knock.
Who's there?
Yah.
Yah who?
Ride 'em cowboy!

Knock, knock.
Who's there?
Ralph.
Ralph who?
Ralph! Ralph!
This is your dog.

Knock, knock.
Who's there?
Tennis.
Tennis who?
Tennis the sum of five added to five.

Knock, knock.
Who's there?
Tamara.
Tamara who?
Tamara is Saturday, no school!

Knock, knock.
Who's there?
Watson.
Watson who?
Watson your mind?

Knock, knock.
Who's there?
Hedda.
Hedda who?
Hedda feeling you were going to ask me that.

Knock, knock.
Who's there?
Passion.
Passion who?
Just Passion my time away
    knocking on doors.

Knock, knock.
Who's there?
Danielle.
Danielle who?
Danielle at me, you started it.

Knock, knock.
Who's there?
Cashew.
Cashew who?
Cashew see it's me?

Knock, knock.
Who's there?
Vaughan.
Vaughan who?
Vaughan day you'll get what's coming to you.

Knock, knock.
Who's there?
Lois.
Lois who?
Lois mark on the test belonged to me.

Knock, knock.
Who's there?
Tank.
Tank who?
You're welcome.

Knock, knock.
Who's there?
Avon.
Avon who?
Avon to be alone.

Knock, knock.
Who's there?
Hatch.
Hatch who?
God bless you.

Knock, knock.
Who's there?
Anna.
Anna who?
Anna going to speak
to you anymore.

Knock, knock.
Who's there?
Butcher.
Butcher who?
Butcher money
where your mouth is.

Knock, knock.
Who's there?
Adore.
Adore who?
Adore stands between us,
    unlock it!

Knock, knock.
Who's there?
Alaska.
Alaska who?
Alaska my mother.

Knock, knock.
Who's there?
Police.
Police who?
Police let me in.
    I have to go to the bathroom.

Knock, knock.
Who's there?
Wyden.
Wyden who?
Wyden you call me last night?

Knock, knock.
Who's there?
Ammonia.
Ammonia who?
Ammonia gonna
    give you one chance.

Knock, knock.
Who's there?
Savannah.
Savannah who?
Savannah you going to show me your report card?

Knock, knock.
Who's there?
Howell.
Howell who?
Howell I get in if you don't know my name?

Knock, knock.
Who's there?
Ida.
Ida who?
Ida better get out of here.

Knock, knock.
Who's there?
Hester.
Hester who?
Hester anyone home?

Knock, knock.
Who's there?
Freddie.
Freddie who?
Freddie or not, here I come!

Knock, knock.
Who's there?
Hugo.
Hugo who?
Hugo first and I'll follow.

Knock, knock.
Who's there?
Oliver.
Oliver who?
Oliver friends will be at the party.

Knock, knock.
Who's there?
Lena.
Lena who?
Lena little closer,
    I want to tell you something.

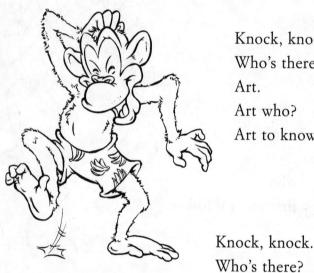

Knock, knock.
Who's there?
Art.
Art who?
Art to know better.

Knock, knock.
Who's there?
Ferris.
Ferris who?
Ferris I'm concerned,
    our friendship is over.

Knock, knock.
Who's there?
Rufus.
Rufus who?
Rufus leaking.
    You better get it fixed.

Knock, knock.
Who's there?
Gorilla.
Gorilla who?
Gorilla cheese sandwich
    for me, please.

Knock, knock.
Who's there?
Omar.
Omar who?
Omar goodness!
    I've lost my wallet.

77

Knock, knock.
Who's there?
Beammie.
Beammie who?
Beammie up, Scottie.

Knock, knock.
Who's there?
Eyesore.
Eyesore who?
Eyesore what you did!

Knock, knock.
Who's there?
Dummy.
Dummy who?
Dummy a favor
    and help me with my homework.

Knock, knock.
Who's there?
Warrior.
Warrior who?
Warrior been all my life?

Knock, knock.
Who's there?
Locker.
Locker who?
Locker up, officer.
She's carrying a weapon.

Knock, knock.
Who's there?
Tilly.
Tilly who?
Tilly-vision is a great form of entertainment.

Knock, knock.
Who's there?
Jamaica.
Jamaica who?
Jamaica call for a taxi? It's here.

Knock, knock.
Who's there?
B.C.
B.C. who?
B.C.'ing you real soon.

Knock, knock.
Who's there?
Matthew.
Matthew who?
Matthew lace has come undone.

Knock, knock.
Who's there?
Disguise.
Disguise who?
Disguise look cloudy today.

Knock, knock.
Who's there?
Hewlett.
Hewlett who?
Hewlett you out of the zoo?

Knock, knock.
Who's there?
Disc.
Disc who?
Disc is a recorded message . . .

Knock, knock.
Who's there?
Isadore.
Isadore who?
Isadore locked? I can't get in.

Knock, knock.
Who's there?
Willis.
Willis who?
Willis be another knock-knock joke?

Knock, knock.
Who's there?
Denial.
Denial who?
Denial's a river in Egypt.

Knock, knock.
Who's there?
Phil.
Phil who?
Phil up the tub with warm water.
   I'm taking a bath.

Knock, knock.
Who's there?
Turnip.
Turnip who?
Turnip the heat,
   Mr. Landlord. I'm freezing!

Knock, knock.
Who's there?
Juan.
Juan who?
Juance upon a time there were three bears....

Knock, knock.
Who's there?
Des.
Des who?
Des are getting longer now that summer is here.

Knock, knock.
Who's there?
Rabbit.
Rabbit who?
Rabbit nice, sir.
It's a gift for my girl.

Knock, knock.
Who's there?
Pecan.
Pecan who?
Pecan somebody your own size!

Knock, knock.
Who's there?
Cook.
Cook who?
Yes, you are crazy!

Knock, knock.
Who's there?
Harry.
Harry who?
Harry up and let's go to the movies.

Knock, knock.
Who's there?
Donkey.
Donkey who?
Donkey very much
   for letting me borrow your skateboard.

Knock, knock.
Who's there?
Jess.
Jess who?
Jess in time. My toes are freezing.

Knock, knock.
Who's there?
Zenka.
Zenka who?
Zenka you
    for being home when I need you.

Knock, knock.
Who's there?
Sherry.
Sherry who?
Sherry argue out here
  or will you let me in?

Knock, knock.
Who's there?
Ozzie.
Ozzie who?
Ozzie you later.

Knock, knock.
Who's there?
Dragon.
Dragon who?
Dragon your feet again, mister?

Knock, knock.
Who's there?
Phyllis.
Phyllis who?
Phyllis in on the latest gossip.

Knock, knock.
Who's there?
Adlai.
Adlai who?
Adlai a bet on my team any time.

Knock, knock.
Who's there?
Ben.
Ben who?
Ben studying
for my math test.

Knock, knock.
Who's there?
Tex.
Tex who?
Tex brains to graduate college.

Knock, knock.
Who's there?
Voodoo.
Voodoo who?
Voodoo you think you're talking to?

Knock, knock.
Who's there?
Boo.
Boo who?
Oh, don't cry,
   it's only me.

Knock, knock.
Who's there?
Fish.
Fish who?
Fish who's are used to blow your nose.

Knock, knock.
Who's there?
Willoughby.
Willoughy who?
Willoughby my friend?

Knock, knock.
Who's there?
Wheelbarrow.
Wheelbarrow who?
Wheelbarrow some money and go out for dinner.

Knock, knock.
Who's there?
Thermos.
Thermos who?
Thermos be a doorbell here somewhere.

Knock, knock.
Who's there?
Osborne.
Osborne who?
Osborne today,
    wish me a happy birthday.

Knock, knock.
Who's there?
Dizzy.
Dizzy who?
Dizzy must be the place!

Knock, knock.
Who's there?
Lion.
Lion who?
Lion in bed last night thinking about you.

Knock, knock.
Who's there?
Buster.
Buster who?
Buster tire so we're gonna have to walk.

Knock, knock.
Who's there?
Myth.
Myth who?
Myth you, too.

Knock, knock.
Who's there?
Alex.
Alex who?
Alex plain later, please open up.

Knock, knock.
Who's there?
Closure.
Closure who?
Closure big mouth,
    or I'll do it for you.

Knock, knock.
Who's there?
Red.
Red who?
Red any good books lately?

Knock, knock.
Who's there?
Sultan.
Sultan who?
Sultan pepper is always used in cooking.

Knock, knock.
Who's there?
Dozen.
Dozen who?
Dozen anyone live here?

Knock, knock.
Who's there?
Agatha.
Agatha who?
Agatha headache.
  Keep it quiet, please.

Knock, knock.
Who's there?
Kojak.
Kojak who?
Kojak up the auto.
    I've got a flat tire.

Knock, knock.
Who's there?
Rover.
Rover who?
It's all Rover between us.

Knock, knock.
Who's there?
Luke.
Luke who?
Luke through the peephole
    and find out.

96

Knock, knock.
Who's there?
Juicy.
Juicy who?
Juicy that movie on TV last night?

Knock, knock.
Who's there?
Snow.
Snow who?
Snow use!
  I can't remember my name.

Knock, knock.
Who's there?
Izzy.
Izzy who?
Izzy home or did he go out?

Knock, knock.
Who's there?
Hurd.
Hurd who?
Hurd the news about cousin Bruce?

Knock, knock.
Who's there?
Alfred.
Alfred who?
Alfred the needle and you can sew my pants.

Knock, knock.
Who's there?
Annetta.
Annetta who?
Annetta joke like this and I'm gone!

Knock, knock.
Who's there?
Pasture.
Pasture who?
Pasture bedtime,
    don't you think?

Knock, knock.
Who's there?
Sharon.
Sharon who?
Sharon share alike.

Knock, knock.
Who's there?
Dawn.
Dawn who?
Dawn you ever answer the door on the first knock?

Knock, knock.
Who's there?
Noah.
Noah who?
Noah good place to go for dinner?

Knock, knock.
Who's there?
Celeste.
Celeste who?
Celeste time I tell you my name.

Knock, knock.
Who's there?
Ringo.
Ringo who?
Ringo round the collar
    is embarrassing.

Knock, knock.
Who's there?
Sizzle.
Sizzle who?
Sizzle be the last time
    I tell you anything.

Knock, knock.
Who's there?
Diplomas.
Diplomas who?
Diplomas here
to fix your pipes.

Knock, knock.
Who's there?
Freighter.
Freighter who?
Freighter me? I'm harmless.

Knock, knock.
Who's there?
Tillie.
Tillie who?
Tillie comes
I'm going to wait here.

Knock, knock.
Who's there?
Frank.
Frank who?
Frank N. Stein.
   Have you seen Igor?

Knock, knock.
Who's there?
Yukon.
Yukon who?
Yukon ask all the questions you like,
   I'm not answering.

Knock, knock.
Who's there?
Kent.
Kent who?
Kent you understand English?

Knock, knock.
Who's there?
Isabel.
Isabel who?
Isabel working or must I always knock?

Knock, knock.
Who's there?
Doughnut.
Doughnut who?
Doughnut open this door until
  you know who it is.

Knock, knock.
Who's there?
Marcella.
Marcella who?
Marcella's full of water.

Knock, knock.
Who's there?
Linda.
Linda who?
Linda helping hand to those who need it.

Knock, knock.
Who's there?
Satin.
Satin who?
Satin the chair and fell asleep.

Knock, knock.
Who's there?
Althea.
Althea who?
Althea tomorrow morning in school.

Knock, knock.
Who's there?
Heaven.
Heaven who?
Heaven heard from you in months.

Knock, knock.
Who's there?
Kip.
Kip who?
Kip it up, wise guy.

Knock, knock.
Who's there?
Annie.
Annie who?
Annie body
    wanna play with me?

Knock, knock.
Who's there?
Who.
Who who?
Do you hear an echo?

Knock, knock.
Who's there?
Stopwatch.
Stopwatch who?
Stopwatch you're saying and think before you speak.

Knock, knock.
Who's there?
Max.
Max who?
Max no difference.
 I'm not staying out here any longer.

Knock, knock.
Who's there?
Franz.
Franz who?
Franz like you
 are hard to come by.

Knock, knock.
Who's there?
Joan.
Joan who?
Joan us for coffee?

Knock, knock.
Who's there?
Major.
Major who?
Major get up, sorry about that.

Knock, knock.
Who's there?
A little kid who can't reach the bell.

Knock, knock.
Who's there?
Date.
Date who?
Date so much for lunch I have a bellyache.

Knock, knock.
Who's there?
Nevin.
Nevin who?
Nevin you mind,
    just let me in.

Knock, knock.
Who's there?
Haydn.
Haydn who?
Haydn seek is a fun game to play.

Knock, knock.
Who's there?
Emma.
Emma who?
Emma new neighbor.
    I just called to introduce myself.

Knock, knock.
Who's there?
Bin.
Bin who?
Bin awhile since you came out to play.

Knock, knock.
Who's there?
Whittle.
Whittle who?
Whittle kids should be seen and not heard.

Knock, knock.
Who's there?
Ashur.
Ashur who?
Ashur hope you recognize me.

Knock, knock.
Who's there?
Dwight.
Dwight who?
Dwight on, brother!

Knock, knock.
Who's there?
Brighton.
Brighton who?
Brighton up your day
and take a walk in the park.

Knock, knock.
Who's there?
Midas.
Midas who?
Midas well listen to me.
I'm a genius!

Knock, knock.
Who's there?
Sanctuary.
Sanctuary who?
Sanctuary much.
The gift was perfect.

Knock, knock.
Who's there?
Genoa.
Genoa who?
Genoa what's happening?

Knock, knock.
Who's there?
Algae.
Algae who?
Algae you in class.

Knock, knock.
Who's there?
Delores.
Delores who?
Delores seeking justice for all.

Knock, knock.
Who's there?
Ice cream.
Ice cream who?
Ice cream if you don't leave me alone!

Knock, knock.
Who's there?
Howard.
Howard who?
Howard you like to stand out here while someone asks,
    "Who's there?"

Knock, knock.
Who's there?
Mohair.
Mohair who?
Mohair is what I need on my head.

Knock, knock.
Who's there?
Custer.
Custer who?
Custer a buck and a half to find out.

Knock, knock.
Who's there?
Waddle.
Waddle who?
Waddle you give me for my old car?

Knock, knock.
Who's there?
Francis.
Francis who?
Francis where they speak French.

Knock, knock.
Who's there?
Ears.
Ears who?
Ears ago I was a little kid.

Knock, knock.
Who's there?
Ken.
Ken who?
Ken I help it
    if you don't recognize me?

Knock, knock.
Who's there?
Razor.
Razor who?
Razor hands
  if you want to leave the room.

Knock, knock.
Who's there?
Scold.
Scold who?
Scold out here.
  Where is my jacket?

Knock, knock.
Who's there?
Alcott.
Alcott who?
Alcott my hair before it gets too long.

Knock, knock.
Who's there?
Olaf.
Olaf who?
Olaf, and I'll puff,
   and I'll blow your house down!

   Knock, knock.
   Who's there?
   Lady.
   Lady who?
   Lady carpet down in the living room.

      Knock, knock.
      Who's there?
      Justice.
      Justice who?
      Justice I thought.
         I'm at the wrong door.

      Knock, knock.
      Who's there?
      Atlas.
      Atlas who?
      Atlas it's Friday,
         no school tomorrow.

Knock, knock.
Who's there?
Jest.
Jest who?
Jest in case you're looking for me, here I am!

Knock, knock.
Who's there?
Thistle.
Thistle who?
Thistle be the last joke you hear from me.

About the Author

ROBERT MYERS was born and raised
in Bronx, New York. He received his
Bachelor's degree from Bernard Baruch
College and his Master's from Jersey City
State College. Mr. Myers is the author of
The Professional Wrestling Trivia Book,
and he currently resides in New York
City with his wife and two children.